Selected Poems
1972–1990

Tom Paulin was born in Leeds in 1949 and grew up in Belfast. He was educated at the universities of Hull and Oxford, and is Reader in Poetry at the University of Nottingham.

TOM PAULIN

Selected Poems
1972–1990

faber and faber
LONDON · BOSTON

First published in 1993
by Faber and Faber Limited
3 Queen Square London WC1N 3AU

Photoset by Wilmaset Ltd, Wirral
Printed in Great Britain by Clays Ltd, St Ives plc

A CIP record for this book is available from the British Library

ISBN 0–571–14941–3

2 4 6 8 10 9 7 5 3 1

For Binday and Jill

Contents

States

That stretch of water, it's always
There for you to cross over
To the other shore, observing
The lights of cities on blackness.

Your army jacket at the rail
Leaks its kapok into a wind
That slices gulls over a dark zero
Waste a cormorant skims through.

Any state, built on such a nature,
Is a metal convenience, its paint
Cheapened by the price of lives
Spent in a public service.

The men who peer out for dawning
Gantries below a basalt beak,
Think their vigils will make something
Clearer, as the cities close

With each other, their security
Threatened but bodied in steel
Polities that clock us safely
Over this dark; freighting us.

Settlers

They cross from Glasgow to a black city
   Of gantries, mills and steeples. They begin to belong.
He manages the Iceworks, is an elder of the Kirk;
   She becomes, briefly, a nurse in Carson's Army.
Some mornings, walking through the company gate,
   He touches the bonnet of a brown lorry.
It is warm. The men watch and say nothing.
   'Queer, how it runs off in the night,'
He says to McCullough, then climbs to his office.
   He stores a warm knowledge on his palm.

   Nightlandings on the Antrim coast, the movement of guns
Now snug in their oiled paper below the floors
   Of sundry kirks and tabernacles in that county.

Under the Eyes

Its retributions work like clockwork
Along murdering miles of terrace-houses
Where someone is saying, 'I am angry,
I am frightened, I am justified.
Every favour, I must repay with interest,
Any slight against myself, the least slip,
Must be balanced out by an exact revenge.'

The city is built on mud and wrath.
Its weather is predicted; its streetlamps
Light up in the glowering, crowded evenings.
Time-switches, ripped from them, are clamped
To sticks of sweet, sweating explosive.
All the machinery of a state
Is a set of scales that squeezes out blood.

Memory is just, too. A complete system
Nothing can surprise. The dead are recalled
From schoolroom afternoons, the hill quarries
Echoing blasts over the secured city;
Or, in a private house, a Judge
Shot in his hallway before his daughter
By a boy who shut his eyes as his hand tightened.

A rain of turds; a pair of eyes; the sky and tears.

Practical Values

Together, or singly, they mean nothing.
How little they have to do with love or care.
The shoaling mackerel, their silver and cobalt;
Perfected girls equipped with cunts and tits;
Soldiers, their guts triggered on wet streets.

Their massed, exact designs are so complete;
Anonymous and identical, they're shaped
By murderous authorities, built like barracks.
Servile and vicious in their uniforms,
In their skins of sleeked metal, these bodies trade.

Thinking of Iceland

Forgetting the second cod war
to go North to that island
— just four days' sailing from Hull —
would be what? An escape?
Or an attempt at finding
what's behind everything?
(bit big the last question for a holiday trip.)

Still, reading the letters
they fired back to England
(one, sadly, to Crossman)
brings back a winter monochrome
of coast and small townships
that are much nearer home:
Doochary, the Rosses, Bloody Foreland.

An empty road over hills
dips under some wind-bent,
scrub trees: there's a bar
painted pink, some houses,
a petrol pump by a shop;
it's permanently out-of-season
here where some people live for some reason.

A cluster too small for a village,
fields waste with grey rocks
that lichens coat — hard skin
spread like frozen cultures,
green, corroded tufts that make dyes
for tweed — shuttles clack
in draughty cottages based in this sour outback.

On the signposts every place
has two names; people live
in a cold climate, a landscape
whose silence denies efforts
no one feels much like making:
when someone is building
it looks like a joke, as though they're having us on.

They poke laughing faces
through fresh wooden struts and throw
a greeting from new rafters;
on the box in the bar
a sponsored programme begins;
the crime rate is low – wee sins
like poaching or drink. It's far to the border.

Now that a small factory
which cans and dries vegetables
has opened, some girls stay
and scour the county for dances.
In these bleak parishes that seem
dissolved in a grey dream
some men are busy mixing concrete, digging septics.

In winter there is work
with the council on the roads,
or with local contractors.
Each year Packy Harkin
builds a new boat, choosing
for a keel a long curving
branch from a sheltered wood where oaks grow straight.

In the dark panelled bar
through the shop, there's a faded
print of an eviction:
one constable crouches
on the thatch, the family stands
at the door, pale, while bands
of constabulary guard the whiskered bailiff.

In the top corner, clumsily,
the face of a young woman
glimmers: *The Irish Patriot,
Miss Maud Gonne.* Sour smell of porter,
clutter of hens in the yard:
no docking in sagaland –
the wish got as far as this coast, then worked inland.

And yet, at Holar, striking matches
in church, trying to snap
a carved altarpiece: strange figures
absent-mindedly slaughtering
prisoners; or 'exchanging politenesses'
with Goering's brother at breakfast,
was this coming-full-circle not the question they asked?

Dawros Parish Church

They stood at the gate before the service started
And talked together in their Glenties suits,
Smiled shyly at the visitors who packed the church
In summer. A passing congregation
Who mostly knew each other, were sometimes fashionable,
Their sons at prep school, the daughters boarding.
Inside it was as neat and tight as a boat.
Stone flags and whitewashed walls, a little brass.
Old Mrs Flewitt played the organ and Mr Alwell
Read the lessons in an accent as sharp as salt.

O Absalom, Absalom, my son,
An hour is too long, there are too many people,
Too many heads and eyes and thoughts that clutter.

Only one moment counted with the lessons
And that was when, the pressure just too much,
You walked slowly out of that packed church
Into bright cold air.
Then, before the recognitions and the talk,
There was an enormous sight of the ocean,
A silent water beyond society.

A New Society

It's easy enough to regret them when they're gone.
Beds creaked on boards in the brick meadows
Somewhere above a tired earth no one had seen
Since Arkwright became a street name.

Their boxed rooms were papered with generations,
There were gas lamps, corner shops that smelt of wrapped bread,
Worn thresholds warmed by the sun and kids playing ball
Near the odd, black, Ford Popular.

Then they were empty like plague streets, their doors barred
And windows zinced. Dead lids weighted with coins,
Dead ends all of them when their families left.
Then broken terraces carried away in skips.

A man squints down a theodolite, others stretch white tapes
Over the humped soil or dig trenches that are like useful graves.
Diesel combusts as yellow bulldozers push earth
With their shields. Piledrivers thud on opened ground.

Just watching this – the laid-out streets, the mixers
Churning cement, the new bricks rising on their foundations –
Makes me want to believe in some undoctrinaire
Statement of what should be. A factual idealism.

A mummified Bentham should flourish in this soil
And unfold an order that's unaggressively civilian,
Where taps gush water into stainless sinks
And there's a smell of fresh paint in sunlit kitchens.

Where rats are destroyed and crawlies discouraged,
Where the Law is glimpsed on occasional traffic duties
And the streets are friendly with surprise recognitions.
Where, besides these, there's a visible water

That lets the sun dazzle on Bank Holidays, and where kids
Can paddle safely. There should be some grass, too,
And the chance of an unremarkable privacy,
A vegetable silence there for the taking.

A Just State

The children of scaffolds obey the Law.
Its memory is perfect, a buggered sun
That heats the dry sands around noon cities
    Where only the men hold hands.

The state's centre terrifies, its frontiers
Are sealed against its enemies. Shouts echo
Through the streets of this angry polity
    Whose waters might be kind.

Its justice is bare wood and limewashed bricks,
Institutional fixtures, uniforms,
The shadows of watchtowers on public squares,
    A hemp noose over a greased trap.

Under a Roof

It'll piss all evening now. From next door
The usual man and woman stuff rants on, then fades;
And I know she'll soon be moaning, climbing her little register
Of ecstasy till quiet settles back like dust,
Like rain, among shadows without furniture.

There was a mattress on bare floorboards when I came,
But now I own a bed, a table, and a chair
In a house where no one knows each other's name,
A zone where gardens overgrow and privet rankles –
It stinks in summer and it blinds the panes.

Cats wail at night among the weeds and bricks,
Prowl rusted fire-escapes that lose themselves
In hedges turned to scrub. Exile in the sticks
Is where I've ended up, under wet slates
Where gas flames dry the air and the meter clicks.

The girl I had scared easily. She saw
The dead bareness of the floor, her body near
Both it and mine, so dressed and left the raw,
Rough room I'd brought her to. Up here I'm free
And know a type of power, a certain kind of law.

Noises, the smell of meals, the sounds that bodies make,
All reach me here, drifting from other rooms.
And what I *know* is how much longer it will take
For thoughts and love to change themselves from these
Than rain and rooms to find their senseless lake.

Incognito

A railway halt a long way from Moscow.
Wide *versts* of flat land and some bunched trees
Smeared dark green by rain blurring the window.
Cold air cut in as she opened it and peered through.
'Look!' she said, 'they've lamps on already,
And they're giving tea there to the engine crew.
What a pity we can't join them, think
Of the warm stove and that samovar!'

He looked up at her face that shone white
In the cold air. It was otherwise dark
In the carriage, and he felt he belonged
To that absence of light.

Ballywaire

My loathsome uncle chews his rasher,
My aunt is mother, pouring tea,
And this is where I live: a town
On the wrong side of the border.

A town the mountain simplifies
To spires and roofs, a bridge that spans
The river – distance shines it – and joins
Packed rural terraces. They're workless,
Costive as the smell of groceries.

Through gunfire, night arrests and searches –
The crossroads loony smashed to bits –
I keep myself intact. My body purifies.
I'll never use it.

The air greys and lights come on
In curtained parlours, our clock ticks
By last year's calendar. The quiet.
An oleograph of Pity in each kitchen.
My heart is stone. I will not budge.

Young Funerals

A nameless visual.
A series of walls, covered windows,
Doors opening into the shared street.
The terrace brings out its dead.

The girl's small coffin, a new glossiness,
Moving through a windy afternoon.

Two doors down, the boy is dying
In his bedroom. It takes months.

When the thin blinds are drawn
I'll hurry past on the other side.
They must not touch me, these deaths.

His parents are names, a different number.
Their front room is photographs and wept shadows,
An empty shop that gives away misery.

Arthur

Everyone's got someone who gave them oranges,
Sovereigns or rubbed florins,
Who wore bottle-green blazers, smoked
A churchwarden pipe on St Swithin's day,
And mulled their ale by dousing red-hot pokers
In quart jars.
But you, you're different.
You pushed off before the millions wrapped their puttees on
And ran away to sea, the prairies, New York
Where they threw you in jail when you told someone
Your blond hair made you a German spy.
After the telegram demanding
Your birth certificate
No one on the Island knew anything about you
Until the Armistice brought a letter
From a wife they'd never heard of.
You'd left her with the baby.
She wanted money.
You were somewhere in South America
In the greatest freedom, the freedom
Of nothing-was-ever-heard-of-him-since.

So I see you sometimes
Paddling up the Orinoco or the River Plate
With rifle, trusty mongrel and native mistress,
Passing cities of abandoned stucco
Draped with lianas and anacondas,
Passing their derelict opera houses
Where Caruso used to warble
Among a million bottles of imported bubbly.

Or else I watch you among the packing-case republics,
Drinking rum at the seafront in Buenos Aires
And waiting for your luck to change;
The warm sticky nights, the news from Europe,
Then the war criminals settling like bats
In the greasy darkness.

Your sister thought she saw your face once
In a crowd scene —
She went to the cinema for a week, watching
For your pale moment. She thinks
You're still alive, sitting back
On the veranda of your hacienda,
My lost great uncle, the blond
Indestructible dare-devil
Who was always playing truant and jumping
Off the harbour wall.

What I want to know is
How you did it.
How you threw off an inherited caution
Or just never knew it.
I think your grave is lost
In the mush of a tropical continent.
You are a memory that blipped out.
And though they named you for the king
Who's supposed to wake and come back
Some day,
I know that if you turned up on my doorstep,
An old sea dog with a worn leather belt
And a face I'd seen somewhere before,
You'd get no welcome.
I'd want you away.

Responsibilities

No way now, there's no way.
Geometry and rose-beds,
The light changing on the hill
Where two gravediggers glance up.
Her tears fell into your silence.

The air starved when the earth pushed.
Something made a fuck of things;
Straight and bare is all it is.
No. I kept you off, my brother,
And I'll never see your face.

Monumental Mason

Working beside a cemetery,
Chiselling dates and names
On cheap slabs of marble
In the lighted shop window,
His meek power makes us nervous.

With his back to the street,
He cuts them in, these loves
The dead can't care about.
In his washed-out overalls
He is less a person

Than a function. People
Have grown used to him
As he sits intently
Gilding the incised letters,
A mason, displayed.

Doris, Beloved Wife
And Mother, or Agnes
RIP, their names are
Public, but we forget them,
Glimpsing a tenderness

On bald stone, some dead letters;
Or, when the traffic lulls,
Hearing from next door
The undertaker's *tap*, *tap*,
Answer his vigilant chinking.

Before History

Mornings when I wake too early.
There is a dead light in the room.
Rain is falling through the darkness
And the yellow lamps of the city
Are flared smudges on the wet roads.
Everyone is sleeping. I envy them.
I lie in a curtained room.
The city is nowhere then.
Somewhere, in a dank *Mitteleuropa*,
I have gone to ground in a hidden street.

This is the long lulled pause
Before history happens,
When the spirit hungers for form,
Knowing that love is as distant
As the guarded capital, knowing
That the tyranny of memories
And factual establishments
Has stretched to its breaking.

Purity

Perhaps a maritime pastoral
Is the form best suited
To a northern capital
With its docks and gantries,
An oil refinery on the salt marsh.

Far from the playful celebration
Of good manners on a green field
There is always that dream
Of duck-down and eider,
The lichened island whose sour light
Lets us be ourselves.

Those luminous privacies
On a bleached coast
Are fierce and authentic,
And some of us believe in them.
They are the polities of love.

But in the brilliant distance
I see a crowded troopship
Moving down the blue lough
On a summer's morning,
Its anal colours
Almost fresh in the sun.
Those black boots are shining.
There is only a pink blur
Of identical features.

Surveillances

In the winter dusk
You see the prison camp
With its blank watchtowers;
It is as inevitable
As the movement of equipment
Or the car that carries you
Towards a violent district.

In the violet light
You watch a helicopter
Circling above the packed houses,
A long beam of light
Probing streets and waste ground.
All this might be happening
Underwater.

And if you would swop its functions
For a culture of bungalows
And light verse,
You know this is one
Of the places you belong in,
And that its public uniform
Has claimed your service.

Traces

They are so light,
Those airmail letters.
Their blueness has fallen
From an Indian sky,
The hot taut atmosphere
Above the muddled village
Your parents write from.

'With God's help,
The crops have been brought
Safely in. All here
Are well, ten *lakhs* of rupees
Our lands are worth now.
That boy's father has twenty acres.
The buffalo are fine,
Though the heat is hard to bear.'

All the fierce passions
Of family and property
Are dictated to a scribe
Who understands English,
Has a daughter to marry
And a dusty handful
Of aluminium coins.

In the Meat-Safe

There is a functional greyness
where the banal, but unusual,
has found a graceless permanence
that only the odd can admire.
Those collectors of cigarette cards
and worthless believe-it-or-not facts,
are the antiquarians of corroded
appliances who worship a dullness
as lonely as the fattest man in the world.

Solemn gaberdines, they cherish
the sweat of broken wirelesses,
goose-pimples on zinc canisters,
pre-war electric razors, sticks
of worn shaving soap, bakelite
gadgets, enemas, ration cards,
contraceptive coils that once fed
safe passions in colourless rooms
chilled by utility furniture.

Most of all they delight in
the stubble that grows on dead chins.
Recording their drab histories
in back issues of *Exchange & Mart*,
they swop this confidence – that,
in the cheap hell of starlets' accents
twittering in faded movies,
someone will sing of tinned kippers
and an ultimate boredom.

Pot Burial

He has married again. His wife
Buys ornaments and places them
On the dark sideboard. Year by year
Her vases and small jugs crowd out
The smiles of the wife who died.

Second-Rate Republics

The dull ripe smell of gas,
A pile of envelopes fading
On the hall table – no one
In this rented atmosphere remembers
The names who once gave this address.

We might be forgotten already,
She thinks, as she climbs the stairs
To spend a long weekend with him.
The trees in these brick avenues
Are showing full and green
Against the windows of partitioned rooms.
The air is humid, and down the street
She hears the single *wuff!*
Of a car door barking shut.

He touches her and she sees herself
Being forced back into a shabby city
Somewhere else in Europe: how clammy
It is, how the crowds press and slacken
On the pavement, shaking photographs
Of a statesman's curdled face.

Now there is only a thin sheet
Between their struggling bodies
And the stained mattress.
Now his face hardens like a photograph,
And in the distance she hears
The forced jubilance of a crowd
That is desolate and obedient.

In the Lost Province

As it comes back, brick by smoky brick,
I say to myself – strange I lived there
And walked those streets. It is the Ormeau Road
On a summer's evening, a haze of absence
Over the caked city, that slumped smell
From the blackened gasworks. Ah, those brick canyons
Where Brookeborough unsheathes a sabre,
Shouting 'No Surrender' from the back of a lorry.

And the sky is a dry purple, and men
Are talking politics in a back room.
Is it too early or too late for change?
Certainly the province is most peaceful.
Who would dream of necessity, the angers
Of Leviathan, or the years of judgement?

The Harbour in the Evening

The bereaved years, they've settled to this
Bay-windowed guest house by the harbour wall.
Each of us loved a man who died,
Then learnt how to be old and seem cheerful.
I think of being young, in the coastguard station.
Those cement cottages with the washing
Swaying in the sea wind. What can she see,
The girl I talk to? Victorian childhoods
Where little stick figures go flickering
Along the roads? Such eagerness that used to be.
A butcher's shop, a boarding house, the dead
Are smiling from the windows there.
So many names, faces, and used things.
Dry calico, the smell of cedar wood . . .
I keep them in a drowsy kind of wisdom.
I have my drawer of rings and photographs.

The waves rustle on the beach like starched silk.
And girls come walking down a staircase
Into a wide room where lamps are burning.
Love was a danger and then children.
At sunset, when I saw the white beacon
On the quay, I felt a tear starting.
But I was happy – like a woman who opens a door
And hears music. It was your face I saw.
I heard your voice, its gentleness.
And I stared over the water at another coast,
An old woman in a sleep of voices.

Line on the Grass

Shadow in the mind,
this is its territory:
a sweep of broken ground
between two guarded towns.

A tank engine rusting
in the long grass, a man
with a fly rod wading
in the grey river.

This looks so fixed, it could
be anytime; but, scanned
in the daylight, the fields
of crops, their hawthorn hedges,

seem too visible. The men
riding black bikes stiffly
along the road are passing
a burnt-out customs post

on an asphalt apron.
They are observed passing,
passing, in a dull light:
civilians at four o'clock.

In the Egyptian Gardens

A white mansion among cypress trees,
You will find histories inside it.
Bronze pins and sheaves of flax,
The dry shadows of a culture.

How many bibles make a Sabbath?
How many girls have disappeared
Down musky avenues of leaves?
It's an autocracy, the past.
Somewhere costive and unchanging.

I love it, but I had to leave.
The rain is falling even now,
And hell is very like those Sunday streets
Where ministers and councillors
Climb out of graves and curse at me.

Anastasia McLaughlin

Her father is sick. He dozes most afternoons.
The nurse makes tea then and scans *The Newsletter*.
She has little to say to his grey daughter
Whose name began a strangeness the years took over.
His trade was flax and yarns, he brought her name
With an ikon and *matrioshka* – gifts for his wife
Who died the year that Carson's statue was unveiled.

McLaughlin is dreaming of a sermon he once heard
From a righteous preacher in a wooden pulpit
Who frowned upon a sinful brotherhood and shouted
The Word of deserts and rainy places where the Just
Are stretched to do the work a hard God sent them for.
His text was taken from the land of Uz
Where men are upright and their farms are walled.

'Though we may make sand to melt in a furnace
And make a mirror of it, we are as shadows
Thrown by a weaver's shuttle: and though we hide ourselves
In desolate cities and in empty houses,
His anger will seek us out till we shall hear
The accent of the destroyer, the sly champing
Of moths busy with the linen in our chests.'

He wakes to a dull afternoon like any other –
The musty dampness of his study, the window panes
That flaw his view of the lawn and settled trees.
The logs in the grate have turned to a soft ash.
The dour gardener who cut them is smoking
In the warm greenhouse, wondering did his nephew
Break in the week before and thieve McLaughlin's silver?

Constables came to the Mill House with alsatians,
And the wet spring was filled with uniforms and statements.
When they found nothing, they suspected everyone.
Even the plain woman who served them tea.
'Father, I am the lost daughter whose name you stole.
Your visions slide across these walls: dry lavender,
Old memories of all that wronged us. I am unkind.'

He sees his son below the bruised Atlantic,
And on a summer's morning in Great Victoria Street
He talks with Thomas Robertson outside the Iceworks.
He sees the north stretched out upon the mountains,
Its dream of fair weather rubbing a bloom on rinsed slates;
He watches the mills prosper and grow derelict,
As he starts his journey to the Finland Station.

Trotsky in Finland

(an incident from his memoirs)

The pension is very quiet. It is called
Rauha, meaning 'peace' in Finnish.
The air is transparent, perfecting
The pine trees and lakes.
He finds himself admiring the stillness
Of a pure landscape. He consumes it.
A bourgeois moment. It might be somewhere Swiss,
The wooden cuckoos calling to an uneventful
Absence, their polyglot puns
Melting in Trieste or Zürich.

The last days of autumn. The Swedish writer
Adds another sonnet to his cycle.
His English mistress drifts through the garden.
An actress, she admires her face
Bloomed in the smooth lake.
At night her giggles and frills dismay
The strictness of minor art.

They leave without paying their bill.

The owner chases them to Helsingfors.
His invisible wife is lying in the room
Above – they must give her champagne
To keep her heart beating, but she dies
While her husband screams for his money.
The head-waiter sets out to find him,
Leaving a crate of gilded bottles
By the corpse upstairs.

                                        The silence here.
A thick snow is falling, the house
Is a dead monument. Insanely traditional.

He is completely alone. At nightfall
The postman carries a storm in his satchel:
The St Petersburg papers, the strike is spreading.
He asks the thin boy for his bill.
He calls for horses. Thinking,
'If this were a fiction, it would be Byron
Riding out of the Tivoli Gardens, his rank
And name set aside. Forced by more than himself.'

He crosses the frontier and speaks
To a massed force at the Institute,

Plunging from stillness into history.

Where Art is a Midwife

In the third decade of March,
A Tuesday in the town of Z –

The censors are on day-release.
They must learn about literature.

There are things called ironies,
Also symbols, which carry meaning.

The types of ambiguity
Are as numerous as the enemies

Of the state. Formal and bourgeois,
Sonnets sing of the old order,

Its lost gardens where white ladies
Are served wine in the subtle shade.

This poem about a bear
Is not a poem about a bear.

It might be termed a satire
On a loyal friend. Do I need

To spell it out? Is it possible
That none of you can understand?

The Impossible Pictures

In this parable of vengeance
There's a spotty newsreel
Being shown inside my head.

What happens is that Lenin's brother
(Aleksandr Ulyanov)
Is being led to execution.

He carries a small book
Wrapped in a piece of cloth.
Is it the Bible or a text

His brother will be forced to write?
He twists it in his hands.
I think he is frightened.

I am wrong, because suddenly
He strikes an officer on the face –
His gestures now are a jerking

Clockwork anachronism.
He is goosestepped to the scaffold.
The frozen yard of the prison

Is like this dawn of rain showers
And heavy lorries, a gull mewling
In its dream of the Atlantic.

Ah, I say, this is Ireland
And my own place, myself.
I see a Georgian rectory

Square in the salt winds
Above a broken coast,
And the sea-birds scattering

Their chill cries: I know
That every revenge is nature,
Always on time, like the waves.

Pings on the Great Globe

A baggy gagman and a rubber duck,
Some bits of eggshell on a dirty plate,
The oilcloth with its scurf of crumbs,
Spilt salt, dried yolk and butter grease.
A litter of newsprint and a stale joke.

Like the snarl of hair burning, its bony pong,
There is a baldness that is brittle.
Unclean! Unclean! The groan of drains,
Their whoop and gritty slabber. Down with
What is done, they glump and splat.

Only the wisest bishop can sit down
To breakfast and call this lovely.
The world is the church of everything
Though an ignorant purity must squat
Among moss and tea leaves in the dank yard.

A Lyric Afterwards

There was a taut dryness all that summer
and you sat each day in the hot garden
until those uniformed comedians
filled the street with their big white ambulance,
fetching you and bringing you back to me.

Far from the sea of ourselves we waited
and prayed for the tight blue silence to give.
In your absence I climbed to a square room
where there were dried flowers, folders of sonnets
and crossword puzzles: call them musical

snuffboxes or mannered anachronisms,
they were all too uselessly intricate,
caskets of the dead spirit. Their bitter
constraints and formal pleasures were a style
of being perfect in despair; they spoke

with the vicious trapped crying of a wren.
But that is changed now, and when I see you
walking by the river, a step from me,
there is this great kindness everywhere:
now in the grace of the world and always.

Under Creon

Rhododendrons growing wild below a mountain
and no long high wall or trees either;
a humped road, bone-dry, with no one –
passing one lough and then another
where water-lilies glazed, primed like traps.

A neapish hour, I searched out gaps
in that imperial shrub: a free voice sang
dissenting green, and syllables spoke
holm oaks by a salt shore, their dark tangs
glistening like Nisus in a night attack.

The daylight gods were never in this place
and I had pressed beyond my usual dusk
to find a cadence for the dead: McCracken,
Hope, the northern starlight, a death mask
and the levelled grave that Biggar traced;

like an epic arming in an olive grove
this was a stringent grief and a form of love.
Maybe one day I'll get the hang of it
and find joy, not justice, in a snapped connection,
that Jacobin oath on the black mountain.

'What Kind of Formation are B Specials?'

The franked letter
lay on the chill tiles
like a writ:
I bent to lift it and saw
this different mark –
magenta and military –
across one corner,
then split the edge and read,
Warszawa 9/12/81.
Yards off, a train leant
on ice and metal,
and I was a zero
in a safe house
asking who was it
crossed the packed snow
with this misdirected, late,
uncandid message
to Anglia, their Anglia?
That fremd evening
I tried to connect
the signs under my eyes
with the state official
who'd scanned your lines,
for now that I've learnt
the oppressor's alphabet
I live in the half-light
of a strange
shivering translation
where the kingdom of letters
is like the postal system

of a frozen state
and your last question
slips through like code.
Now I go down
among the glubbed carp
of catholic Europe
that taste of mud and penance
this Christmas Eve,
and in the belly
of a non-nation
admire a chosen hunger . . .
but I still can't pray,
end, or send this letter.

Desertmartin

At noon, in the dead centre of a faith,
Between Draperstown and Magherafelt,
This bitter village shows the flag
In a baked absolute September light.
Here the Word has withered to a few
Parched certainties, and the charred stubble
Tightens like a black belt, a crop of Bibles.

Because this is the territory of the Law
I drive across it with a powerless knowledge –
The owl of Minerva in a hired car.
A Jock squaddy glances down the street
And grins, happy and expendable,
Like a brass cartridge. He is a useful thing,
Almost at home, and yet not quite, not quite.

It's a limed nest, this place. I see a plain
Presbyterian grace sour, then harden,
As a free strenuous spirit changes
To a servile defiance that whines and shrieks
For the bondage of the letter: it shouts
For the Big Man to lead his wee people
To a clean white prison, their scorched tomorrow.

Masculine Islam, the rule of the Just,
Egyptian sand dunes and geometry,
A theology of rifle-butts and executions:
These are the places where the spirit dies.
And now, in Desertmartin's sandy light,
I see a culture of twigs and bird-shit
Waving a gaudy flag it loves and curses.

As a White Lodge in a Garden of Cucumbers

Voluble in a slum,
in a garlic opera
where paper roses
fall from a tarnished ceiling
and the room smells
of roasting ptarmigan,
capsicums, and songs
juicy as peaches,

these lazy painters
have slipped off
to take a sly poke
at every pedagogue.
It is time, they sing,
to praise the surface,
the pure and twisting
figure-of-eight that curves

the sun within itself.
They strip to irony
and clever laughter
in a comedy of oil.
Hilarious, his prong;
what a scream her fanny is;
though the senna teacher
squeaks, why aren't they serious?

Descendancy

All those family histories
are like sucking a polo mint –
you're pulled right through
this tight wee sphincter
that loses you.
e.g. I've a second cousin
drives a prowl car
in downtown Vancouver,
and another's the local rozzer
in a place called Buxton.
Could be that a third one
– say an ex-B Special –
has pulled up at a roadblock
a shade far from Garrison?

The Book of Juniper

In the original liturgy
on a bare island

a voice seeks an answer
in the sea wind:

'The tides parted and I crossed
barefoot to Inishkeel.

Where was the lost crozier
among the scorched bracken?

And where was that freshet
of sweet water?

Goose-grass and broken walls
were all my sanctuary,

I mistook a drowsed hour
for the spirit's joy;

on a thymy headland
I entered

the strict soul
of a dry cricket.

Heat haze and wild flowers,
a warm chirring all

that civil afternoon,
till its classic song

failed me and I sighed
for a different love

in grey weather.'
*
'Place the yeasty word
between my lips,

give me comfort
in a sheepfold,

shelter me
in a mild grove.'
*
'There is no word
and no comfort.

Only a lichened stone
is given you,

and juniper,
green juniper.'
*
Tougher than the wind
it keeps a low profile
on rough ground.
Rugged, fecund,
with resined spines,
the gymnosperm
hugs the hillside
and wills its own survival.
The subtle arts are still to happen
and in the eye of a needle
a singing voice
tells a miniature epic
of the boreal forest:

[47]

not a silk tapestry
of fierce folk
warring on the tundra
or making exquisite love
on a starry counterpane,
but an in-the-beginning
was a wintry light
and *juniperus*.

*

On the brown hills
above a Roman spa
in Austro-Hungaria
the savin hides
its berries of blue wax
in a thorny crown,
while in the rapt
shaded casino
a small black ball
skips and ricochets
like a sniper's bullet.

Jug-ears and jowls,
walrus moustaches, frowns –
those gravid urns
on clotted mahogany.
What mineral water can soothe
a tetchy liver or a glum colon?

The wheel flicks,
the hard pea itches;
in the gummed hotel
fingers dibble and thrust
like sappers pushing
through primed earth.

Later, the dry scrape
of an empty tumbler
locked on a ouija board
will spell out a dead yes
like chalk on a billiard cue.

The wind riffles the savin;
the humid band begins to play.

*

A clear and tearful fluid,
the bittersweet *genièvre*
is held to a wet window
above a college garden.

On the lazy shores
of a tideless sea,
the Phoenician juniper
burns a fragrant incense
in a sandy nest.

And in a Zen garden
all the miniature trees
have the perfect despair
of bound feet.

Exiled in Voronezh
the leavening priest of the Word
receives the Host on his tongue –
frost, stars, a dark berry,
and the sun is buried at midnight.

*

On a bruised coast
I crush a blue bead
between my fingers,
tracing the scent, somewhere,
of that warm mnemonic haybox,

burnished fields, a linen picnic
and a summer dawn
where mushrooms raise their domed gills.
They are white in the dew
and this nordic grape
whets an eager moment
of bodies meeting in a fishy fume.
Its meek astringency is distilled
into perfume and medicines,
it matches venison
as the sour gooseberry
cuts the oily mackerel.
Spicy, glaucous,
its branches fan out
like the wind's shadow
on long grass,
then melt back
and go to ground
where swart choughs
open their red beaks,
stinging the air
with stony voices.

*

Though it might be a simple
decoration
or a chill fragrance
in a snug souterrain,
I must grasp again
how its green
springy resistance
ducks its head down and skirts
the warped polities of other trees
bent in the Atlantic wind.

For no one knows
if nature allowed it
to grow tall
what proud grace
the juniper tree might show
that flared, once, like fire
along the hills.

*

On this coast
it is the only
tree of freedom
to be found,
and I imagine
that a swelling army is marching
from Memory Harbour and Killala
carrying branches
of green juniper.

Consider
the gothic zigzags
and brisk formations
that square to meet
the green tide rising
through Mayo and Antrim,

now dream
of that sweet
equal republic
where the juniper
talks to the oak,
the thistle,
the bandaged elm,
and the jolly jolly chestnut.

Argument from Design

Your glooby voice
is salt and carrageen,
a dolphin fountain
among the bay trees
in a Tuscan garden
where a dwarf on a tortoise
guards the pearly grotto;
and your quaint frizz
has this ebony wrinkle
glazed with bruised purple,
an aubergine lip,
a barbel-beard.
What a baroque smörgåsbord!
bad taste of the blond north
doing a flip
with the sugars of the deep south.

Off the Back of a Lorry

A zippo lighter
and a quilted jacket,
two rednecks troughing
in a gleamy diner,
the flinty chipmarks
on a white enamel pail,
Paisley putting pen to paper
in Crumlin jail,
a jumbo double
fried peanut butter
sandwich Elvis scoffed
during the last
diapered days —
they're more than tacky,
these pured fictions,
and like the small ads
in a country paper
they build a gritty
sort of prod baroque
I must return to
like my own boke.

A Rum Cove, a Stout Cove

On the Barrack Islands far out
in the South Atlantic
the great-great-grandson (Sol Grout)
of Nelson's last bosun
is packing crawfish into a thick
barnacled keepbox marked *Briton
Kanning Factors Illimitated*.
It's his swart locks and cochin cheeks
that glim in the top left-hand corner
of 'Bold Bessie', the prime banner
that longs to LOL 301.
Like Gib, like the god called M'Lud,
and those tars behind locked doors
whistling *Britannia Rules*
in their slow skrimshandering
with worn and corded tools,
he's firm, Sol Grout, to the core,
the genius of these used islands
where no maritime elegists sing
of Resolution or Independence
with their harbourmaster's stores,
clagged mountains of ashy shale
and a small bird that no one has named –
a flightless timorous landrail
whose cry is rusted, hard, like chains.

A Written Answer

This poem by Rupert Brookeborough
is all about fishing and the stout B-men
(they live for always in our hearts,
their only crime was being loyal),
there is a lough in it and stacks of rivers,
also a brave wee hymn to the sten-gun.
The poet describes Gough of the Curragh
and by his use of many metric arts
he designs a fictionary universe
which has its own laws and isn't quite
the same as this place that we call real.
His use of metonymy is pretty desperate
and the green symbolism's a contradiction,
but I like his image of the elm and chestnut,
for to me this author is a fly man
and the critics yonder say his work is alright.

Manichean Geography I

Consider a coral or guano atoll
Where a breezy Union Jack
Flaps above the police station.

There is a rusting mission hut
Built out of flattened tin cans
(Bully beef, beans and tomato pilchards)

Where the Reverend Bungo Buller
And his prophet, Joe Gimlet,
Preach the gospel of cargoes.

They worship a white god
Of dentures and worn toothbrushes
Who will come to earth, Hallelulia,

In a reconditioned Flying Fortress
Humping bales of fresh calico
And a crate of Black and Deckers.

Seeding like brisk parachutes,
The ancestral spirits will fall
From the pod of an airship,

And the chosen people will serve
Themselves with orange jube-jubes
In a brand-new discount warehouse.

Manichean Geography II

Banal hours in muggy weather.
The slack wind – warm, trammelled –
Is named for a freighter
That dumped its clotted chains
In Prince Darling Bay.
One time, sometime, never again old chug.

From a rainwood pulpit
The Reverend Spanner McTavish
Preaches a burnt sermon
On the injustice of the Copra Board
While an Anglican head-hunter
Reads *Phrenology Made Easy*
And fidgets with his namba.
One time, sometime, never again old chug.

Sunset and a frigate-bird
Circling the chalk lighthouse.
In a twilight of flying foxes
The coconut crabs are shredding
O-level papers in English Literature,
As a pidgin ode is chanted
In the deepy rainforest
To a signed photograph
Of his High Troppo Majesty
The Duke of Edinburgh.
One time, sometime, never again old chug.

To bossy saltmen from wayback
The islands are a spatched necklace
Of prickly heat, boils,
And choggy boredom.
Big Ben Man, where is?
Asks the girl whose white teeth
Have the blank snowy dazzle
Of coconut flesh.
Just look what we've made
Of your damned islands, we answer.
They are images now
– Never again old chug –
Images of our own disgust.

L'Envie de Commencement

Dactyls and the light of harbours:
how simple it is in the beginning
for the historian to walk at dawn,
seeing a pure narrative before him.

Local Histories

A khaki bell-tent in the mopane forest:
Professor 'Deeko' Kerr is on vacation
Observing the delicate birds of Africa.
He leaves his russet hide to take a leak,
'What I have, I hold,' he thinks as the boy
Sneaks a quick gander at his pinko prong.
Chit-chat evaporates at this charred altitude
Like letters airmailed to Great Namaland
Or Deeko's postcards to his old headmaster
Who wrote the school would be most pleased to learn
Of his promotion to the Chair of Social Justice
At Jan Smuts College in the Orange Free State.
He thanked him also for his learned article,
'Samuel Twaddell: a Co. Down Man at the Cape'.
Even now, at a bring-and-buy in Cleaver Park,
His Aunt Mina is telling Lady Lowry,
'That boy's gone far, but we've heard nothing yet.'

A Daily Beauty

Before he emigrated to Philadelphia, John Dunlap, the printer
of the Declaration of Independence, was an apprentice in Gray's
printing-shop in Main Street.

A tray of waspy plums and American apples,
three yards of cracked oilcloth tacked to the counter,
that mild pong of ham, pan loaves, the paraffin tang
of newsprint from a stack of sisalled papers:
the *Derry Journal*, *Weekly News*, and *Strabane Chronicle*.
It's buzzy slapdash in and out: a private's squatting
on an elsan in the sangar by the humpy bridge,
as *Bannigan's Gravels* rakes through its gear-box
and the auctioneer's voice drills the clabbery market
like a scorching lark over a prison yard.
There's Union Street and Barrack Street, and here's me
just an ignoramus with a jammy piece,
taking a holyer in these slurried townlands.

Presbyterian Study

A lantern-ceiling and quiet.
I climb here often and stare
At the scoured desk by the window,
The journal open
At a date and conscience.

It is a room without song
That believes in flint, salt,
And new bread rising
Like a people who share
A dream of grace and reason.

A bit starchy perhaps.
A shade chill, like a draper's shop.
But choosing the free way,
Not the formal,
And warming the walls with its knowing.

Memory is a moist seed
And a praise here, for they live,
Those linen saints, lithe radicals,
In the bottled light
Of this limewashed shrine.

Hardly a schoolroom remembers
Their obstinate rebellion;
Provincial historians
Scratch circles on the sand,
And still, with dingy smiles,

We wait on nature,
Our jackets a dungy pattern
Of mud and snapped leaves,
Our state a jacked corpse
Committed to the deep.

Of Difference Does it Make

During the 51-year existence of the Northern Ireland Parliament only one Bill sponsored by a non-Unionist member was ever passed.

Among the plovers and the stonechats
protected by the Wild Birds Act
of nineteen-hundred-and-thirty-one,
there is a rare stint called the notawhit
that has a schisty flight-call, like the chough's.
Notawhit notawhit notawhit
– it raps out a sharp code-sign
like a mild and patient prisoner
pecking through granite with a teaspoon.

Amphion

Flame on the salt marsh,
thin chimney
like a pen, or a pencil,
it makes the surface
a planished thing
and burns, tribeless now,
over the slobland.

On a concrete apron
by the slack perimeter,
there is a line of surplus trucks,
nine gross of jerricans
under a pegged tarpaulin,
and a stack of exhaust pipes
wrapped in waxed paper.
A short man in an overcoat –
the new government auctioneer –
waddles, stops, and waddles on
like a dumpy general.

Over the road
on reclaimed space
and dry dumped earth,
there is that pointed,
unpainted sense
of real absence
that bites like a beginning.

Ah, we say, this is culture —
the flame, the hardware
and a voice
that imagines what it describes
and draws from the earth and the air
this new-strung form
that betters what we are.

S/He

There's burnt ground
and a cindertrack
all along the ridge
between the shops
and the railway bridge,
like it's occupied territory
with no one around
this cold snap.
Here's a wet sheugh
smells like a used sheath,
and here's frogspawn
and a car battery
under a screggy hawthorn.
They're having a geg
chucking *weebits* and *yuk*
and laughing at the blups –
kids turned fierce
on a tip,
little hard men in boiler suits
locked in a wargame.

Yesterday I stared
at this girl with cropped hair –
a grandpa shirt on her
and lovebites on her neck,
little pinky bruises
like a rope had snagged there.

Ah shite, the bitter joy
as the plunged head gets born! –
a March wind
hits the main street
of a village called Convoy
and I'm starved
by the first screech that's torn
from out the guts of the blind poet.

*

Something in the air,
too-quiet-altogether
on the back road that slips
down into Derry.
Where that open pasture
slopes from a close wood
to a file of chestnuts
there's a counterfeit sense
that unsettles me just now.
It might be the landlord's absence
from a version of pastoral,
or the hidden scanner
that has to be somewhere.

Over the ramp
the light that bangs back
from the fieldgrey screens
has a preserved feel to it,
like radio silence
or the site of an accident.

I wind down the window,
pass proof of myself
and match
the copper stubble on his chin
with the light green
of his shirt –
may God forgive me
this parched gift of sight.

*

This hereness is to loiter
by a quay in Derry
and gaze at the spread river,
the pigeons and the pigeon-cowlings
on a stained flour mill,
until a voice whispers
in the balmy sigh of a lover,
'who's in the wrong county
like the maiden city?'

*

'Would you give us a lift, love?
it's that late n'scary . . .'
I was only half there
like a girl after a dance,
wary, on the road to Muff.
We might've been out after curfew
in the buzzy *deux-chevaux*,
slipping past the chestnuts
on a street in provincial France.

It stuck close to me, though,
how all through the last half
a helicopter held itself
above the Guildhall –
Vershinin's lines were slewed
by the blind chopping blades,
though Olga looked chuffed
when she sighed, 'Won't it be odd
with no soldiers on the streets?'

Ceremony

I see the women come walking
From the town of the white river-meadow.
Their eyes are a silk fragrance;
Their ritual must appease
The squat god, Terminus.

One is shy and delicate
As she carries a bowl of wine;
And another, in the spirit's beauty,
Will transfigure the hard god
With honey on a green leaf.

He hunches at the stone bridge,
A crude surplus taskman
In a blocked sangar. His raw
Fur is grey and hackled,
His broody vigilance

The shadow of all judgement.
Rain and lichens
Have weathered him, and now
He squats like an institution –
Useful, half-wise, no longer young.

Honeyed wine and spicy cakes,
A fluid light and a fine
Twist of air – a song is rising
To a gold-bellied sail
That takes, takes and quickens us.

To the Linen Hall

After extremity
art turns social
and it's more than fashion
to voice the word *we*.
The epic yawp
hangs like an echo
of the big bang,
though now we tell children
to shun that original –
primal light, soaked green,
the slob mud
and a salt tang.
There is a ban
on philosophies of blood,
a terse demand
for arts and skills
to be understood,
and a common flow
into the new academy
which rules with a chill,
strenuous and insistent,
enforced formality.
Here we have a form
and a control
that is our own,
and on the stone steps
of that eighteenth-century,
reasoned library
we catch the classic spore
of Gibbon and new *ceps*,

the busts and statues
that might be stored
under the squares.
Our shaping brightness
is a style and discipline
that finds its tongue
in the woody desk-dawns
of fretting scholars
who pray, invisibly,
to taste the true vine
and hum gently
in holy sweetness.

The Bungalow on the Unapproved Road

The mattress on their bed
was so spongy
we fell all night
into a cut-price nothing
that wrecked our backs.
The headboard was padded
with black vinyl –
just the ugliest thing
I'd seen in a long time,
though the new wallpaper
they'd bought in Wellworths –
tequila sunsets
on the Costa Brava –
might take the biscuit.
That May morning
I looked out at the Bluestacks
and the Glen River –
a wet, chittering
smash of light
where a black Vauxhall
jeuked round a bend
on jammy springs,
like a patched Oldsmobile
heading for Donegal
with a raft of hooch in the trunk.

An English Writer on the French Revolution

His book is dedicated
to certain ladies –
Mrs John Rae
and Mrs Clive Street
who compiled the index
and served tea
under a damson tree.
He tells us that Barère
was left-handed
and owned a small library
of Chinese pornography
which he called
mon cabinet noir.
He tells us the exact size
of Fouquier-Tinville's
ear trumpet,
argues that Chénier
was a foot taller
than his brother
and describes the operation
on the Dauphin's foreskin.
He is building a bridge
from here to Betelgeuse –
a bridge of damson stones,
tin trumpets
and left testicles.
I sit under my vine
and read him gently.

Waftage: An Irregular Ode

All my mates
were out of town
that lunk July
and though we shared a bed still
it was over.
She'd paid the rent
till August first
so each bum hour
those rooms chucked back at me
this boxed-up, gummy warmth
like a pollack's head and eye
wedged in an ironstone wall.

Most every day
she'd paint
in the loft above the stables
while I wandered
right through Le Carré –
Murder of Quality
was where I started.
That dower-house,
it felt like a forced holiday
or some queer, white theatre
open but empty
on the Sabbath.

At night we'd mount
this slippy mime
called *Boffe de politesse* –
we did it best
in the bath, I reckon –
a kind of maritime
bored experiment,
all yompy farts
and soap torpedoes.
One dayclean, though,
when a pouter-dove
was crooling

like a soft hoor,
I thought how James Fenton
read Shakespeare in Saigon –
got the complete works
in dime paperbacks
on the black market.
Bit by bit he'd foreground
the subterfugue text
within the text itself,
and so turn wiser –
aye, I used think wiser –
than us boneheads here.

It was quiet
in the Circus;
Bill Haydon wafted
down a corridor . . .
For a geg one day
I bought this tin
of panties coloured
like the Union Jack,
but she slung it in the bin
and never breathed
the least bit sigh.
'*Va-t'en!*' she spat,

'I just can't stand you.
No one can.
Your breath stinks
and your taste
it's simply foul –
like that accent.
Please don't come slouching
near my bed again.'
So, real cool, I growled
'Lady, no way you'll walk
right over *me*.'
Dead on. I chucked her then.

Peacetime

We moved house
in '63.

My brother cried
quietly in his room.

Stuff in the loft,
my dad said burn it.

I cut the brass buttons
from his khaki tunic,

sploshed petrol,
felt in the back pocket

of the heavy trousers –
no wallet,

only four sheets
of folded bog-roll

(he'd been an officer
and planned ahead).

I chucked a match.
Whap!

Fivemiletown

The release of putting off
who and where we've come from,
then meeting in this room
with no clothes on –
to believe in nothing,
to be nothing.

Before you could reach out
to touch my hand
I went to the end of that first
empty motorway
in a transit van
packed with gauze sacks
of onions.
I waited in groundmist
by a hedge
that was webbed with little frost nets –
pointlessly early
and on edge,
it was like rubbing one finger
along the dulled blade
of a penknife,
then snapping it shut.
I need only go back,
though all of my life
was pitched in the risk
of seeing and touching you.

A church and a creamery,
the trope of villages
on the slow road to Enniskillen
where they made a stramash
of the Imperial Hotel
two days before
our last prime minister
was whipped to Brize Norton
at smokefall.

When I found the guest-house
opposite Byrne's Hardware
the girl, Bridie, said 'Nah,
she's not back yet –
d'you want wait on her?'
But I went off
down the main street
like the place was watching
this gaberdine stranger
who'd never seen it before.

There was a newish wood
above a small, still lough
so I climbed into its
margin of larch and chestnut,
one of those buck eejits
that feels misunderstood –
the pious, dogged friend
who's brought just comfort,
no more than that.

I smoked a cigarette
while an olive armoured car
nosed down the hill –
no more than I could, it'd never fit
the manor house's *porte cochère*
and white oriel,
for I felt dwammy sick
at the fact of meeting you again
so near and far from home
and never saying
let's run from every one of them.
There was a half-hour
when I could still
slip back to The Velma
and leave a note with her –
I called but you weren't in.
See you.

Rosetta Stone

We were real good
and got to share a desk
that smelt like the head's Bible
when I lifted up its lid
and nicked a sharp HB
from Eileen's leather pouch,
knowing that she knew
but would never tell on me.
There wasn't a single hair
between our sleeping legs
that I could ever see –
only that spiky *différance*
waiting on history.
Hers was a little plum,
mine a scaldy that could pee
yella as the tartan skirt
she slid one tiny bit
to let me touch her pumice-silk,
chalky like my glans might be.

Symbolum

after Johann Wolfgang von Goethe

The mason lives
in this or that street
and all his actions
are like yours or mine.
He makes us equal.

He sees loose clouds
like a bishop's jowls
and the furred stars
that should be even –
king superstitions.

But he'll go out
with spirit-level,
square and trowel
to plant a ladder
on this earth.

The sun shines
on his foundations –
a pentagram
cut in packed soil,
the bricks stacked ready.

Calque

I got up and went downstairs –
that was the first act
        waxy and banal
        of the day
now the entire room had this
        set smell
        cold tobacco say
except that estranged phrase
it turned me right off
like an owl had gone *cucu*
out in the cleared day
        and the light
        that light
        all cold clean buyable
        Hardware River
        wrapped in cello
        or some kinda sap
don't they all wear the same fucking clothes?
        oh my head's sore
        there's just no aura
        OK so it's repro OK
but every last bitta this is me

Voronezh

(Anna Akhmatova)

You walk on permafrost
in these streets.
The town's silly and heavy
like a glass paperweight
stuck on a desk –
a wide steel one
glib as this pavement.
I trimp on ice,
the sledges skitter and slip.
Crows are crowding the poplars,
and St Peter's of Voronezh
is an acidgreen dome
fizzing in the flecked light.
The earth's stout as a bell –
it hums like that battle
on the Field of Snipes.
Lord let each poplar
take the shape of a wine-glass
and I'll make it ring
as though the priest's wed us.
But that tin lamp
on the poet's table
was watched last night –
Judas and the Word
are stalking each other
through this scroggy town
where every line has three stresses
and only the one word, *dark*.

Mythologies

I like that story with its thoughtful prisoner,
miles of salt marsh and a word like *wesh*
I could never figure –
those chalk sticks making buckled letters
                on slates the colour
                of a schoolgirl's knickers
then the sour cloth you wiped the slate with.
There was something in it, too,
                about a jack –
jack-knife, jack-towel, jack,
                words for lawyers
                perhaps
                or dead geraniums
                waiting to be topped.
I read it in my oral childhood –
                some daft ould map
                had joined the Farcet's mouth
                to the mainland
so I could cross that bridge like Satan
                and hide among
                the British people
not noticing their love of dog-smells
                fairgrounds
                pub signs
                smoked dukes
most anything at all with bottom in it.
Also the stadiums where they moan and thresh
                they moan and sigh
                like knobby forests.

For this was like an almost-love
                some love you never chose
                you wipe your nose just
                come back for more
                and print neat lies.

'There are many wonders on this earth'

Chorus from Antigone

There are many wonders on this earth
and man has made the most of them,
though only death has baffled him
he owns the universe, the stars,
sput satellites and great societies.

Fish pip inside his radar screens
and foals kick out of a syringe:
he bounces on the dusty moon
and chases clouds about the sky
so they can dip on sterile ground.

By pushing harder every way,
by risking everything he loves,
he makes us better, day by day:
we call this progress and it shows
we're damned near perfect!

Breez Marine

It was my birthday
in the Europort
a Polish barber
cut my hair so short
that a young squaddy
came blinking out
– chin smooth
legs unsteady –
into that glazed street
they call Coldharbour.
We waited three minutes
by the photobooth
– some early warning –
and me and her
we fought a battle
'bout my hair
and my blue passport.
She laughed at me
by that barbarous pole
so rudely forced
and when the wet prints
slid through the hole
shrieked *just as well*
we'll never marry
would y'look at those?
Each stunned eye
it shone like a dog's nose
pointing at a prison dinner.

All I could try
was turn a sly
hurt look to soften her
and that night in bed
I stuck my winedark tongue
inside her bum
her blackhaired Irish bum
repeating in my head
his father's prayer
to shite and onions.
But my summum pulchrum
said *I've had enough*
we rubbed each other up
a brave long while
that's never love.

I Am Nature

Homage to Jackson Pollock, 1912–56

I might be the real
>Leroy McCoy
>landsurveyor
>way out west
>of Gila River

you know I pushed my
>soft bap
>out her funky vulva
>her black thighs
>and my first cry
>was Scotch–Irish
>a scrake
>a scratch
>a *screighulaidh*

I passed nights

>sidewinding
>on the desert floor
>fertil arid zone
>smoke trees
>creosote bush
>ironwood
>Joshua trees

till I lit
                    on dreamtime
                    wrote my nose
                    in sand
                    the infants'
                    burying-ground

I did learn for sure there
                    smoketaste
                    piñon
                    chicken flesh
                    mesquite

and turned wise
                    as sagebrush

smart as the tabs
                    on a 6-pack
                    as cat's claw
                    chickenwire
                    thorn

I flicked fast through the switches
                    licking her oils
                    blood gunge
                    paintjuice
                    gumbo
                    Stella McClure
                    off of my skin

rubbed all of them back but
                    hear me sister!
                    brother believe me!

just banging on
                    like a bee in a tin
                    like the burning bush

[93]

cracking dipping and dancing
                like I'm the last
                real Hurrican Higgin
                critter and Cruthin
                scouther and skitter
                witness witness
                WITNESS TREE!

An Ulster Unionist Walks the Streets of London

All that Friday
there was no flag –
no Union Jack,
no tricolour –
on the governor's mansion.
I waited outside the gate-lodge,
waited like a dog
in my own province
till a policeman brought me
a signed paper.
Was I meant to beg
and be grateful?
I sat on the breakfast-shuttle and I called –
I called out loud –
to the three Hebrew children
for I know at this time
there is neither prince, prophet, nor leader –
there is no power
we can call our own.
I grabbed a fast black –
ack, I caught a taxi –
to Kentish Town,
then walked the streets
like a half-foreigner
among the London Irish.
What does it feel like?
I wanted ask them –
what does it feel like
to be a child of that nation?

But I went underground
to the Strangers' House –
We vouch, they swore,
We deem, they cried,
till I said, 'Out . . .
I may go out that door
and walk the streets
searching my own people.'

Why the Good Lord Must Persecute Me

I don't visit this noticeboard much
— the one in my study
maybe you only look at them
when you're in real need
— there's a list or a timetable
some piece of printed stuff
that orders you to do
or to be something
but I keep one picture
pinned to the black cork
— CALVIN FAREL
each theologian
is let into a wall
like a long thin clock
— fierce *féroce* feral stiff
a pair of stone pricks
or the boots I dig with
  my brain's gonging now
I've just had a liquid shite
then juice coffee a horrible suck
of black caporal
now now now I'll unfold a chair
and stare at that high terrible scooped smooth
rational wall
between my eye and the water jet
all the while I'm leafing through
The History of Received Opinions
— see this, the word *tradition*
it'll squeak if you touch it
then break up like a baked turd

into tiny wee bits
and here's a missing chapter
that tells what you can't rub out
however much you might want to

Really Naff

He'd cropped hair
and a sweater –
a tight one on bare skin.
Something too full about the face
but shy with it.
A bit like a tope –
a tope or an airplane
if you seen them from above.
There was this warning flag
at the quarry –
someone's underpants strung on a pole
by a concrete hut.
I felt the blast stub the hill
then we climbed up a track
past Lough Free they call it.
We drove home the next day.
My eyes were wide open,
I stared down –
it's the thrash of new love –
at these scribbly lines
in the Ormeau Baths.
I notched his neck with my lips.
In bed he was all thumbs –
I was jabbed like a doorbell –
until he collapsed
sticky with the promise
of making my bum.
Which he didn't.

So I call him Mr Thumb
and draw eyes on that face
with a felt tip –
flat as a pancake
or a kid's drawing.
I put in ocean, fathoms, light,
but he's as bare as need, poor guy,
or the sole of that trainer.

The Defenestration of Hillsborough

Here we are on a window ledge
with the idea of race.

All our victories
were defeats really

and the tea chests in that room
aren't packed with books.

The door's locked on us
so we begin again

with cack on the sill
and *The Book of Analogies*.

It falls open at a map
of the small nations of Europe,

it has a Lutheran engraving
of Woodrow Wilson's homestead

in a cloon above Strabane,
and it tells you Tomáš Masaryk

was a locksmith's apprentice.
This means we have a choice:

either to jump or get pushed.

The Caravans on Lüneburg Heath

one of those unlucky Fridays, Simon,
    a bust-up, dirty time to be alive
writing an elegy for the pumpkin hut and *Gärtchens*
without your neat metre and full rhymes

what I have to say's dead obvious
    we've had x years of blood and shit
    and some of us have written poems
    or issued too many credos through the press

    Simplex plays the pipe indeed
    But the soldiers pay no heed.

waiting a contact watching the normals
in the quick frame of their street lives
. . . cigarette butts carriers bus passes ackhello
they lie whole weeks in attics
wire potato clamps
or kit themselves in aprons and straw hats
knowing the natural order
for the vigilant fake it is

I'm watching three young butchers
dressed up as themselves
it's a hot new lunchtime
in the town of Newry
they camp through the market look

then break triangulate gap

you'll hear the shots like instant recollection

Simplex sees the squad car stop –
Four young men have got the chop.

*

it took us a few years only to grow that house
on a bit of land the town council give us
a cultured place beside the River Pregel
where we read out poems to each other
hoping that Zion's daughter
was maybe a presence in our speech
– surely she'd help us shelter from the rain?

other people that concept we grew up with
they made us out a pack of tubes
our heads full of gourds pumpkins squashes peppers
we treated cucumbers like art objects
and loved the slippy gunge that cauls the melon seeds
every stranger was made welcome in our house
you brought a bottle or a spondee and got tight
you cast your bread upon the waters of the Pregel
and things came back to you that primal happiness
before you turned like Christ upon the mother
sangar blockhouse lookout post OP
you made a garden in its place
a cultivated man turning the earth and raking soil
till it smells like new cord and you press the seeds in

*

Simon you're the It that isn't there
you're the reader and the writer
the crowd's buzz

a sizzly shifting block of midges
as I trailed one hand in the Pregel
or trailed it in the Pregolya
a river named during a wet lunch at Potsdam

sugar furs saltfish copper sandstone corn
so many commodities things being moved
through the Holy Roman Empire of the German Nation
hard to tell what would happen
as the Empire burst like a bag
and logs slipped downriver
to the papermills at Königsberg

how many years back were Slavata and Martinitz
pushed out of that window?
at what hour of the night was it in Ruzyn
or Hradčany Castle they hanged Slansky?
thousands of statements dropped from the presses
and the day I read Kant's starry sentence
on a bronze tablet in Kaliningrad
my protestant faith in the printed text
turned back on itself

Tilly Wallenstein the spider Spinola
Gustavus Ferdinand Charles
Colonel Horn working the Lauterbach Valley
how scrupulous the sense of landscape is
in every description of armies before a battle

the flat sandy soil scrubby woods holm oak and larch
the narrow marshy streams slick oily water
between Rocroy and Rumigny
the lagoons and salt marshes of East Prussia
Simon I sometimes believe it's us poor saps
gives each of these places its strange and exact presence
as if we're part of the action though the whole bloody mess
it doesn't depend on our minds just
for the chosen ground is always packed
with skulls in section norns some end result

*

we cracked too many bottles
in our fuggy bower
we smoked and made mantalk in the small hours
we cut our girls' names on pumpkins and melons
– *Arsille Rosita Emilie*
the letters distorted as they grew
and our writing stopped being ours

cucumber leaves furred with wee spines
like glasspaper or emery skins
you could polish furniture with the dry ones
or stroke one finger over their crinkly pumice
I imagined marketing them like poems
each one the slow rub of high culture
waxing a chairback's wooden pelvis

so I dreamed and wanked in a cage of swelling vegetables
each living graffito mocking my prick's ikons
riverboats passed trailing music like vines
each name went its own way left me behind
the place is a wreck now I just hurry past it
looking for signs of age in myself the used voice
the creased pouchy face on a coathanger
understudy for that weddingcake left out in the rain

half truths cagey handshakes those lyrics written
to your own sadness and tight esteem
I cling to my friends like soft rain on bar windows
I don't believe God is much interested
in this or that country what happens or doesn't
and after twenty odd years breaking lives like firewood
is there anything can shock us now?
the Virgin of Magdeburg charred in a ditch
the sleeping girl they shot because she married out
why give a shit if what you write doesn't last?

[105]

could you feel could you really feel any joy
watching the nation states rising up like maggots?

*

the West's last thinker, part woodcutter
and part charlatan
is digging trenches on the Rhine
                    — lonely uncanny violent
                    the artist and the leader
                    without expedients
                    apolis
                    without structure and order
                    among all that is —
in the summer of '44
a memo named me the most expendable
member of my university

I was thankful digging
this will be useful to me
like an alibi
I was thinkful dagging
in the firebreak
the firebreak between armed forests
Herr Professor
must keep his head down
                    — bridge and hangar
                    stadium and factory
                    are buildings
                    but they're not dwellings
                    Bahnhof und Autobahn
                    Staudamm und Markthalle
                    sind Bauten
                    aber keine Wohnungen —

if I refused to drop
three Jews from the faculty
had I not praised
Totenbaum
rooftree
coffin
tree of the dead
— a farmhouse in the Black Forest
built two centuries back
by the dwelling of peasants?
as I praised the Führer
it was like all the dead feet
walked into our room
where my wife stood by the fire
cleaning my hairbrush
and I complained to her
about that thin singed aftersmell
its bony frazzle and suddenness

                              *

he digs deep in the earth
or stands with small tight goggles against the snowglare
a survivor like you and me
outside the ski hut at Todtnauberg
this old smooth fuck
tried stare through history
at the very worst moment

> *Simplex watched the committee men*
> *Shuffle, mumble and give in.*

without conscience
the day they buried Husserl's ashes
I kept to a ribbed path
and listened to the forest
its silent tidal boom

the all cave of language
and I heard him
Masaryk's teacher
as I watched the Rhine
'a wordy digger
is not the worthy digger
of his own grave
you're one of those small fry
who funked my sickroom'
days after he died
I'd written Frau Husserl
'forgive me
I should have stated
my admiration and my gratitude'
then I dropped the dedication
Sein und Zeit
was as clean as its title
a set text
the pages resinous
as pine laths
knocked into a box
and the missing name of Edmund Husserl
rosepink like a knot
or the eye of a white mouse

this red Rhine clay
lignite and gravel
Grund
I stood on the wet
ontic particles
my boots sogged
in muddy water
fires luffed
on the other bank

fires the French had lit
I bribed a guard
and had six nights
on a mudbank in a *toten Arm*
one hour before dawn
on day seven
I crossed their lines
coffee and a visa
Bolivia Paraguay anyplace
what wouldn't I have given
for just those two things?
but the lieutenant's face
was the face of a student
tensing in a seminar
der kleine Judenbube
from NYU

'Go chew acorns
Mr Heidegger
you went with the Nazis'

thrown into a place
unstable here and nowness
a forest pope who lived
on the quiet side of the stink
I answer
if others did worse
they did worse
but some felt guilt
guilt is not my subject

male corpses
floating downriver
in white winter battledress
the wide melting root

of Germany
they weren't my fault
one hundred metres of piano wire
the July plotters
noosed in a warehouse
I might've sat in that courtroom
next Helmut Schmidt
a uniformed observer
postponing speech

I was watching the Rhine
as a sealed truck
powered by wood gas
jupped through the forest
I never saw it
nudge the gates of Flossenbürg
never watched them
take that pastor to the gallows

Bonhoeffer Bonhoeffer
is this then *meine Schuld*?

*

> *Simplex sees the final strike*
> *Devastate that evil Reich.*
> *Simplex says I'm going now*
> *You can read this anyhow.*

*

water's twisting down the hillsides in long sheets
all I can say is they fought over the same places
      Alpine passes
      Rhine crossings
      Regensburg bridgehead
      Magdeburg bridgehead
      the plains of Leipzig and Brabant

easy to say it now the war's long over
but you'll find me Simon an idea only
where five khaki caravans are parked on a heath

I'll follow in the Field Marshal's shadow
an orderly an illusion that crosses
ling tyretracks crushed grass
to feel in the left pouch of its battledress
for a pen that'll pass like a baton
from one officer to the next

we unfold ten chairs and a table
in the shabby tent by the flagpole
it's inside/outside
chill temporary
like a field latrine

he keeps their delegation waiting
then draws them up
under the Union Jack
tying back a flap
I notice three brown buds on a twig
all gummy and glycerine

von Friedeburg their naval commander
he wept during lunch I wiped glasses
and held them up to the canvas light
they signed the instrument of surrender
then lit cigarettes the way young people used to
after sex in the daytime

*

now I can get born again
as a square of tracing paper
in A B or C block

flats brickfields cindertracks
it's 9 a.m.
some Monday in February
a building by a muddy river
on a postwar island

onestorey partitioned
tacked out of hardboard
and scrap fuselage
this aluminum school
is split in four sections

lines radiate
in from each pupil
and one tight thread
links *Lüneburger Heide*
to the Clogher Valley
– provincial world history
or the seedbed of soldiers

Dill Alexander
Montgomery Alanbrooke
they're crimped on my brain tissue
like patents or postcodes
their building's the hard rectangle
that kitted me out first
as a blue British citizen

which signifies only
that this flattened trashcan
has more than enough room
for Tommy's wee collection
of aesthetic judgements

decals
further descriptions
loony tunes
or Free State referenda

so in all this melt
of incident and hot metal
there's still time to stop over
on the road to Damascus
— a light a voice patch of stamped earth
and if you ask my opinion now
I'll tell you about our musical *Kürbishütte*
then hand you a cucumber
and say it doesn't exist

'Winds and rivers'

Winds and rivers,
light, sea, earth, winds,
wind on the needlegrass
and light,
light on the greased eel and the greyhound,
I call on you –
on the pure and the slimy,
the running, shotsilk
skim of you –
I call on you as witnesses
to my first millennium
as Zeus's prisoner.
Didn't I make things happen?
Didn't I seize the fire of ideas
and make them leap, tear, fly, sing –
the rush and whap of them
in each split moment! –
and now I can do nothing,
nothing will happen.
Mortal, ashamed, cowed, frightened –
clamped to its frozen edges,
the humans hugged the earth
and waited for wipe-out.
The secret source of fire and heat –
that one, primal,
Idea of all ideas,
I searched it out –
so delicate and brittle
I hid it in a cusp of fennel,

a single spark
inside that aromatic
greeny-white bulb.
I swam like a mullet
with a hook bedded
in its soft mouth –
I swam
in the smell of the ocean,
in the huge dazzle of all ideas
and always hearing
just as I'm hearing now
the quick fluster of seabirds flying.

'The gods of our new mythology'

PROMETHEUS

The gods of our new mythology are all generals and
politicians. I helped them get power. I watched them drive in
stretched limos to ceremonies where they made speeches and
then awarded each other honours, titles, medals, stars, brownie
points. And always there was some historian handling the
press. Down on the ground the people humped heavy loads
and suffered back pains and self-disgust. Those humans
drudged. They'd no idea what they were for. Witless, glum,
trapped, they blundered about with their heads down. So I
gave them the idea of skill – first the deftness of hands
working, then the *techne* of making objects out of wood, clay,
stone and bone. Then the smelt of soft and tough metals, until
they could find in the glow of fire what came first and before
all these new arts – the idea of mind. All I felt was an immense
patience and good will. Toward everything human I felt
friendly. There was nothing alien or strange about the small
gnarled artefacts they began to skrimshander out of
whalebone, teak, black soapstone. Little gods, animals kissing,
keepsakes, bison running, white horses – they began to make
images and objects, each with its own aura. When first they
started they had eyes but didn't yet know how to look at the
world. Their ears were blocked by wax and ignorance, lies that
had been stuffed there. I taught them different. They lived in
holes and grim caves, not knowing how to build houses or
even make bricks. Time and the seasons, the movement of stars
and planets, they could measure none of these things. The
abstract beauty of pure number, the designing of signs on
paper, the infinite accounts in memory banks – they knew

[116]

nothing of these. I taught them to sail, fly, glide and push themselves out at the stars – but look at me, stuck here, I can't escape. I was free to refuse my talents, but I gave them, gave them generously.

'Holy Mother, Themis, Earth'

PROMETHEUS
Holy Mother, Themis, Earth,
it must all break
here in this wet yard
at the world's end
where they design pain
in secret for me
and cross my name –
my whole nature out –
by writing REBEL
then mocking me for what I'm not.
Men, women, tiny kids,
every juicy little life –
Zeus wanted crush them.
I heard their stittering
frantic cries,
cries like pebbles bouncing
on a stone floor,
and my conviction
was simple and complete.
That's why I stole
that restless, bursting,
tight germ of fire,
and chucked its flames
like a splatter of raw paint
against his state.

They seized the running trails
and ran with them,
every mind fizzing like resin –
racing, dancing, leaping free,
jumping up into the sky,
and nudging deep
into the ocean's bottom.
Every mind was a splinter
of sharp, pure fire
that needled him
and made him rock
uneasy on his throne.
See Zeus, shaken
as these new lights burn
and melt his walls.
Let Prometheus go out
and become one
with the democratic light!

Note

'The Caravans on Lüneburg Heath'

Simon Dach (1605–59) was professor of poetry in Königsberg and the most important figure in the Königsberg circle of poets. His poem, 'Klage über den endlichen Untergang und Ruinirung der Musicalischen Kürbs-Hütte und Gärtchens. 13. Jan. 1641', was first published in 1936. It is printed in the selection of seventeenth-century poems in Günter Grass's novella, *Das Treffen in Telgte*, which is set near the end of the Thirty Years War. 'The Caravans on Lüneburg Heath' is loosely based on Simon Dach's 'Lament over the Final Demise and Ruination of the Musical "Pumpkin Hut" and the Little Garden' and is also indebted to *The Meeting at Telgte*, Ralph Manheim's translation of Grass's novella. Manheim translates 'Kürbs-Hütte' as 'Cucumber Lodge/Bower' and notes the allusion to Isaiah 1:8 – 'And the daughter of Zion is left as a cottage in a vineyard, as a lodge in a garden of cucumbers, as a besieged city.' Manheim also explains that Cucumber Lodge was an informal Königsberg literary society which used to meet in the poet Heinrich Albert's garden in a bower overgrown with cucumbers. There they would sing their own songs set to music by Albert.

I have also drawn on various essays by Martin Heidegger and on certain evasive, and probably mendacious, public statments which Heidegger issued in order to justify his conduct under the Nazi regime. I have drawn, too, on Paul Celan's poem to Heidegger, 'Todtnauberg'.